Victim Assistance

(Law Enforcement and Judicial System Information)

a resource booklet

By

Richard L. Robinson

ISBN: 1-4140-1029-X (e-book)
ISBN: 1-4140-1028-1 (Paperback)

This book is printed on acid free paper.

1stBooks - rev. 02/12/04

VICTIM ASSISTANCE

Law Enforcement and Judicial System Information

A Resource Booklet by

Richard L. Robinson, Executive Director of **TIPS KID'S CARE ASSOCIATION** [non-profit educational resource center]

THIS EDUCATIONAL BOOKLET IS FOR

- The Public at Large
- Anyone arrested
- Victim Assistance Program
- Family members of anyone arrested
- Crime Prevention Program

- Religious organizations
- Witness of Crime — Penology System
- International travelers
- Immigrants
- Learning institutions

AND

FOR THOSE WHO DO NOT KNOW HOW THE CRIMINAL JUSTICE SYSTEM WORKS WITH REGARD TO:

- Obtaining an Arrest Warrant
- Being Arrested
- Being Released
- Bond Arraignment
- Sentencing
- Detention Facility Purpose and Jail Purpose
- Parole
- Probation
- Preliminary Hearings
- Pre-Trial Invention Program
- Arrest Warrants
- Bench Warrants
- Public Defender Representatives
- Medical Costs for Inmates
- General Sessions Bench Warrants

- Bondsmen
- Roll Call for General Session Court
- "Weekender" Sentences
- Housing of Inmates
- Arrest Behavior
- Fraudulent Checks
- Child Support Payments
- Juvenile Arrest Policies
- Violent Crime Control and Law Enforcement Act
- Judicial Appointments
- Criminal Domestic Violence Act
- Inmate Privileges
- Criminal Justice System Terminology
- Court Charges Categories

A   Informative assistance reference resource guidelines on Law Enforcement and Judicial System Information booklet that every household in America and international travelers need to have on hand as a reference booklet should a family member or friend be arrested on a particular criminal arrest warrant charge.

B   Not knowing what to do to get a family member or friend released from jail or Detention Center may cause you and your family excessive spending and grief.

C An educational informative resource booklet that is easy to read and self-explanatory about law enforcement and judicial information in the American criminal justice system.

Law Enforcement and Judicial System Information

THE 1997 VICTIM AND WITNESS SERVICE STATUTE

A VICTIM OR WITNESS HAS THE FOLLOWING RIGHTS:

1. To be treated with fairness, respect and dignity and to be free from intimidation, harassment, or abuse and informed of a victim's constitutional rights.
2. To be reasonably informed when the accused or convicted person is arrested, released from custody, or has escaped.
3. To be informed and present at all criminal proceedings which are dispositive of the charges where the defendant has the right to be present
4. To be allowed to submit either a written or oral statement at all hearings affecting bond or bail.
5. To be heard at any proceeding involving a post-arrest, a plea, or sentencing.
6. To be reasonably protected from the accused or persons acting on his behalf throughout the criminal justice process.
7. To confer with the prosecution after the crime against the victim has been charged, before the trial, or before any disposition, and informed of the disposition.
8. To have reasonable access after the conclusion of the criminal investigation to all documents relating to the crime against the victim before trial.
9. To receive prompt and full restitution from the convicted person or persons.
10. To be informed of any proceeding when any post-conviction action is being considered, and be present at any hearing.
11. To a reasonable disposition and prompt and final conclusion of the case.

Sentence Codes & Guideline Information Relating to Criminal Arrest Warrant Charges
(Guideline Information may vary from state to state)

- Failure to support spouse and children (Code 2007-90); Felony (E): 1 year and/or $300-$6,500.
- Involuntary manslaughter (Code 16-3-60); Felony (F) Sentence time is 5 years.
- Homicide by child abuse causing death (Code 16-3-85); Felony (c) Sentence time is 20 years-
- Life.
- Lynching, 1st degree (Code 16-3-210); Felony Sentence time is Death or 5-40 years with recommendation of mercy.
- Lynching, 2nd degree (Code 16-3-220); Felony Sentence time is 20 years.
- Assault with concealed weapon (Code 16-3-610); Misdemeanor (c) Sentence time 1 year or fine
- (Amount is discretion of court).
- Spousal sexual battery (Code 16-3-615); Misdemeanor (C) Sentence time is 10 years.
- Assault and battery with intent to kill (Code 16-3-620); Felony (E) Sentence time is 20 years.
- Resisting Arrest with a deadly weapon, 1st (Code 16-3-620); Felony (E) Sentence time is 20 years.
- Criminal sexual conduct, 3rd (Code 16-3-654); Felony (E) Sentence time is 10 years.
- Criminal sexual conduct with minor (Victim 11-14) (Victim 16); Felony (c) Sentence time is 20 years.
- Violent; possible life sentence.
- Engaging child under 18 for sexual performance (Code 16-3-810); Felony (C) Sentence time 20 years.
- Kidnapping (Code 16-3-910); Felony (A) Sentence time is 30 years. Violent, possible life sentence.
- Threatening life of public official (Code 16-3-1040); Felony (F) Sentence time is 5 years.
- Stalking, 1st; No temporary restraining.
- Order/Injunction in effect (Code 16-3-1070); Misdemeanor (C) Sentence time is 1 year and/or $1,000.
- Stalking, 1st Temporary restraining order.
- Injunction in effect (Code 16-3-1070); Misdemeanor (B) Sentence time is 3 years and/or $5,000.
- Criminal domestic violence, 1st and 2nd (Code 16-25-30); Sentence time is 30 days or $500.
- Criminal domestic violence, 3rd (Codes 16-35-20 & 16-25-40); Sentence time is 3 years and/or $3,000.
- Lewd act on a minor (Code 16-15-140); Felony (D) Sentence time is 15 years and/or fine (amount is discretion of court).
- Carjacking, without great bodily injury (Code 16-3-1075); Sentence time is 15 years.
- Carjacking, with great bodily injury (Code 16-3-1075); Felony (B) Sentence time is 25 years.

- Engaging in riot, no weapon involved/no injury (Code 16-5-120); Misdemeanor Sentence time is 30 days or $100.
- Assault on police office while resisting arrest (Code 16-9-320); Misdemeanor (C) Sentence time is
- 10 years and/or $1,000-$10,000.
- Aiding escape of prisoners under sentence (Code 16-9-410); Felony (E) Sentence time is 10 years.
- Aiding escape from prison, non-capital offenses (Code 16-9-410); Misdemeanor (B) Sentence time
- is 2 years or $500.
- Aiding escape from custody of officers (Code 16-9-420); Misdemeanor (B) Sentence time is 2 years or $500.
- Arson, 3rd (Code 16-11-110); Felon (C) Sentence time is 10 years.
- Arson, 2nd (Code 16-11-110); Felony (B) Sentence time is 20 years.
- Arson, 1st (Code 16-11-110); Felony (A) Sentence time is 25 years.
- False claim to obtain insurance benefits, fire or explosion loss (Code 16-11-125); Felony (F)
- Sentence time is 5 years and/or $10,000.
- Burglary, 1st (Code 16-11-311); Felony Sentence time is 15 years-Life.
- Burglary, 2nd (Code 16-11-312); Felony Sentence time is 15 years.
- Burglary, 3rd (Code 16-11-313); Felony (A) Sentence time is 10-30 years.
- Armed robbery (Code 16-11-330); Felony (A) Sentence time is 10-30 years.
- Common law robbery (Code 16-11-325); Felony (D) Sentence time is 15 years.
- Attempted armed robbery (Code 16-11-330); Felony (C) Sentence time is 20 years.

THE FOLLOWING IS NOT MEANT TO BE ALL INCLUSIVE. I AM SURE THAT WE WILL FIND OTHER OFFENSES THAT NEED TO BE INCLUDED. REMEMBER, THE VICTIM IN THE CRIME MUST BE AN INDIVIDUAL BEFORE THE LAW APPLIES.

Victim and Witness Services Offenses

Abandonment/children

Abuse/neglect/child/vulnerable adult

Accessory to these offenses

Administering/Attempt to poison

Arson/all degrees

Any assault or assault/battery

Assisting in hazing

Attempt to do these offenses

Armed robbery

BOT>$1000 and up

Breaking into auto

Burglary/all degrees

Burning land/crops

Carjacking

Common law robbery/strong arm robbery

Communicating obscene message/not telephone

Computer Crime Act violations {not 3rd degree. 1st offense

Conspiracy t do these offenses

Contributing to the delinquency of a minor

Criminal domestic violence

Criminal receipt of goods fraudulently obtained

Criminals sexual conduct—all degrees

Cruelty to children

Cultivating marijuana on land of other

Cutting/removing timber without permission>$50 and up

Damaging/destroying by incendiary device — all

Deceptive sale of fuel/oil

Dueling/challenging/second to

Denial of equal enjoyment/privilege-public accommodation

Denial of mental health patient's rights

Discharging firearm into dwelling

Disclosing mentally ill patient's records

Discrimination in treatment of prisoners

Disposal of stored cotton

Disseminating obscene material/show to minor - all

Disturbance of worship services

Disturbing schools

Eavesdropping/peeping tom

Employing person<18-nudity/to violate obscenity law

Enticing child to be truant

Entry land of others 3rd offense

Entry without breaking to steal

Exploitation of vulnerable adult

Exposing other to HIV virus

Extortion

Failure of officer to protect property from riot

Failure to lay laborer > $100

Failure to report abuse/neglect/exploitation—vulnerable adult

Failure to support spouse/children

False imprisonment

Financial transaction card theft

Forgery

Harassment

Highway robbery

Homicide by child abuse

Illegal use of stink bomb

Incest

Indecent exposure

Intimidation of witness/official

Involuntary manslaughter

Kidnapping

Killing by poison/stabbing/duel

Larceny $1000 end up-all types

Lewd act on minor

Lynching

MIPP/MIRP > $1000 and up

Malicious injury - place of worship

Making/branding/disfiguring large animal of another

Mayhem

Medically indigent assistance act confidentiality violation

Murder

Obstructing RR - death or injury to person

Obtaining property by false paper or pretenses > $1000 and up

Prostitution of minor

Pointing/presenting firearm

Possession of dangerous animal which attacks a human

Possession of firearm/knife during crime of violence

Possession of stolen vehicle >$1000

Robbery after entering train

Robbery/vehicle for hire operators

Safecracking

Seduction under promise of marriage

Sexual exploitation of minor

Sexual intercourse with patient/trainee at mental institute

Slender/libel

Spousal sexual battery

Stalking

Stealing crops >$1000 and up from field

Swindling

Taking hostage by inmate

Threatening life of public official

Threatening voter

Threaten to kill/damage by incendiary device

Transporting child < 16 out of state/violation of custody order

Unlawful conduct towards child

Unlawful use of telephone

Use of vehicle without permission

Violation of order of protection

Voluntary manslaughter

Willful/malicious attempt to burn

Willful violation of consumer protection code

Willful violation of RR law resulting in injury

- Malicious injury to real property, $1,000.01 (Code 16-11-520); Sentence time is 5 years or fine (amount is discretion of court).
- Malicious injury to personal property, $1,000 (Code 16-11-510); Sentence time is 30 days or $500.
- Larceny, $1,000 (Code 16-13-30; Misdemeanor (c) Sentence time is 30 days or $500.
- Shoplifting, $1,000 (Code 16-1 3-110) Sentence time is 30 days or $500.
- Purse snatching (Code 16.13-150); Misdemeanor (A) Sentence time is 3 years.
- Breach of trust, $1,000 (Code 16-13-230); Sentence time is 30 days or $500.
- Obtaining property by false pretenses, $1,000.01 (Code 16-13-240); Sentence time is 5 years of Fine (amount is discretion of court).
- Carrying concealed weapon (Code 16-23.460); Misdemeanor Sentence time is 30-90 days or $200-$500.

<u>Traffic Sentence Codes & Guideline Information Relating to Criminal Arrest Warrant Charges</u>
(Guideline Information may vary from state to state)

- Alteration Etc. of vehicle identification number (Code 56-29-30); Felony (F) sentence time is 5 years and/or $5,000-$10,000.
- Driving under suspension, license not suspended for DUI, 1st (Code 56-1-460); Sentence time is 30 days or $200.
- Driving under suspension, license suspended for DUI, 1st (Code 56-1-460) Sentence time is 10-30 days.
- Driving under suspension, license not suspended for DUI, 2nd (Code 56-1-460); Sentence time is 60 days and $500.
- Driving under suspension, license not suspended for DUI, 3rd + (Code 56-1-460); Sentence time is 90 days-6 months.
- Driving under suspension, license suspended for DUI, 3rd + (Code 56-1-460); Sentence time is 6 months-3 years.
- Driving under the influence, 1st (Code 56-5-2930); Sentence time is (1) 48 hours-30 days or 48 hours public service or (2) $200.
- Driving under the influence, 2nd (Code 56-5-2930); Sentence time is (1) 48 hours-1 year or 10 days public service and (2)$2,000-$5,000.
- Driving under the influence, 3rd (Code 56-5-2930); Sentence time is 60 days-3 years and $3,500-$6,000.
- Felony driving under the influence and death results; Felony (B) Sentence time is 1-25 years and $10,000-$25,000.
- Operating uninsured motor vehicle, 1st Sentence time is 30 days or $100).

Note: *All criminal arrest warrant charges listed on these pages can be reduced or lowered on sentence time and fines by the presiding judge who is handling that particular arrest warrant case, by law.*

Some of the information in this resource booklet footnoted as being from the *South Carolina Criminal Justice Academy's Jail Officer Training Manual* originally appeared in the *National Sheriffs' Association Manual for Law Enforcement Officers.* Permission for use has been kindly granted by author Mr. Aldine N. Moser Jr., Executive Director of the *National Sheriffs' Association.* A Special 'thank you' to Mr. Moser on behalf of Tips *for Kids' Care Association.*

A portion of the proceeds from the sale of this resource booklet will go toward the financial support and responsibilities of the T*ips for Kids' Care Association* located in Spartanburg, South Carolina — a non-profit child development educational information-resource service. The Tips *for Kids' Care Association* was established to provide quality updated and advanced learning and skills materials published by County, State and Federal learning resource agencies and institutions to parents, students, and various child development and education units within this great country.

Acknowledgments

To the Creator

To my parents — Mrs. Virginia Robinson and the late Mr. Willie Robinson Jr.

To my Grandmothers — The late Irene Sanders and Ethel Robinson

To my brothers — John W. Robinson, Gerry Robinson, Steve Robinson

To my only sister — Tracy A. Moore

To relatives — Uncle John Williams, Aunt Ruth, all my nieces, nephews, and cousins

To special friends:

- Warden Larry Powers — for giving me a professional employment opportunity as a Detention Officer, a position in which to learn to apply Law Enforcement skills and knowledge to better serve humankind and the community at large.

- Dr. Joyce A. Miller — A classmate, many thanks for writing the *Preface* to this resource booklet.

- Nine Star Publications and my Literary Consultant, Cyn Massey

For guidance:

- My humble thanks to God for sharing the vision and knowledge, and in helping me put this valuable information into a booklet for the public at large for its assistance with the Judicial system.

- My Mother, Mrs. Virginia Robinson — my special love and appreciation for her spiritual guidance.

For kind words, support, encouragement:

Without the loving support, encouragement, end understanding of my dear wife, my mother, children, brothers, sisters,
Elijah Williams, Mr. William Velasco, Captain Speller, Cpl. Melvin, Sgt. Waff, Officer Dunn, and other Officers of the Spartanburg County Detention Center, Administrative Resources, Donna Ezell and Staff, Doug Brackett, Harold D. McClain, Captin Freeman, Reverend Peter Jones, Brenda Lee, and Hudson Barksdale, Jr.,
I would not have been able to complete this work.

My deepest gratitude to each and all, and any who I inadvertantly may not have mentioned.

Also, a special note of thanks to Aldine N. Moser, Jr., Executive Director of the National Sheriffs' Association - 1450 Duke Street - Alexandria, Virginia 22314-3490.

If, by any chance I have omitted anyone, please forgive me — Richard L. Robinson

Dedication

The booklet is dedicated to the many professional men and women of the different agencies of Law Enforcement within this country, solicitors and judges, staff members and representatives who often perform a seemingly thankless job in the face of great stress and something danger.

A special note of thanks goes to my wife, Janette, and my two sons, Maurice and Derrick, who have put up with many nights of "Daddy working late" to assemble this material. To each of them I offer my thanks, love, and understanding.

Richard L. Robinson

CDR Codes - Common Drug Offenses

POSSESSION:

0659 MARIJUANA 1ST (0-30 days or $100-200)
0182 MARIJUANA 2ND {0-1 yr &or S200-1K}
0176 COCAINE/LSD/HEROIN (other narcotic) 1ST {0-2yrs&or $0-5K} &or $5K+}
0177 COCAINE/LSD/HEROIN (other narcotic) 2ND {0-5yrs &or $0-5K}
0178 COCAINE/LSD/HEROIN (other narcotic) 3RD {0-5yrs &or S0-10K}

0179 OTHER sched I-V 1ST (0-6 months & or $0-1K)
0180 OTHER sched I-V 2ND {0-1 yr &or $0-2K}
0100 CRACK/CLANK 1ST {0-5yrs
0101 CRACK/CLANK 2ND{0-10yrs or $10K+}
0102 CRACK/CRANK 3RD{10-15yrs &or $15K-}

DISTRIBUTION & PWID:

0183 COCAINE/LSD/HEROIN (other narcotic) 1ST {0-15yrs &or S0-25K}
0184 COCAINE/LSD/HEROIN (other narcotic) 2ND [SER] {5-30yrs &or $0-50K}
0185 COCAINE/SD/LSD/HEROIN (other narcotic)3RD (SER) (15-30yrs &orS0-50K)
0186 sched I-III (includes MJ) 1ST{0-5yrs &or 50-5K}
0187 sched I-III (includes MJ) 2ND {0-10yrs &or S0-10K}
0188 sched I-III (includes MJ) {5-20yrs &or S0-20K}
0179 MARIJUANA OVER 1oz 1ST {0-6 MONTHS &OR $0-1K}
0180 MARIJUANA OVER 1oz 2ND {0-1 yrs &or $0-2k}

0112 CRACK/CRANK 1ST {0-15yrs &or$25K-}
0113 CRACK/CRANK 2ND{10-25yrs &$50K-}
0114 CRACK/CRANK 3RD (ser) {0-30yrs & $100K-}
0189 sched IV 1ST {0-3yrs &or S0-3K}
0190 sched IV 2ND {0-5yrs &or S0-6K}
0191 sched V 1ST {0-1yrs &or S0-1K}
0192 sched 2ND {0-2YRS &or S0-2k}

TRAFFICKING: [all are violent and serious]

0278 COCAINE (10-28 grams) 1ST {3-10yrs & $25K}
0387 COCAINE (10-28 grams) 2ND {5-30 yrs & $50K}
0147 COCAINE (10-28 grams) 3RD {25-30 YRS & $50K}
2359 COCAINE (28-100 grams) 1ST {7-25 yrs & $50K}
0388 COCAINE (28-100 grams) 2ND {7-30 yrs & $50K}
0148 COCAINE (28-100 grams) {25 yrs & $100K}
0280 COCAINE (100-200 grams) {25 yrs & $50K}
0288 COCAINE (200-400 grams){25 yrs & $100K}
0281 COCAINE (400 or more grams){25-30 yrs & $200K}
2361 HEROIN (4-14 grams) 1ST {7-25 yrs & $50K}
0156 HEROIN (4-14 grams) 2ND {25 yrs & $100K}
0287 HEROIN (4-28 grams) 1ST {25 yrs & $200K}
0149 HEROIN (4-28 grams) 2ND {25-40 yrs & $200K}

0450 CRACK/CLANK (10-28 grams) 1ST {3-10 yrs &$25K}
0451 CRACK/CLANK (10-28 grams) 2ND{5-30 yrs & $50K}
0349 CRACK/CLANK (10-28 grams) 3RD {25-30 yrs & $50K}
0392 CRACK/CLANK (28-100 grams) 1ST {7-25 yrs & $50K}
0389 CRACK/CLANK (28-100 grams) 2ND (7-30 yrs & $50K}
0349 CRACK/CLANK (28-100 grams) {25-30 yrs & $50K}
0368 CRACK/CLANK (100-200 grams) {25 yrs & $50K}
0369 CRACK/CLANK (200-400 grams){25 yrs & $100K}
0370 CRACK/CLANK (400 or more grams){25-30 yrs & $200K}
2360 MARIJUANA (10-100 lbs) 1ST {1-10 yrs & $10K}
0402 MARIJUANA (10-100 lbs) 2ND {50-20 yrs & $15K}
0145 MARIJUANA (10-100 lbs) 3RD {25 yrs & $25K}

OTHER:

0296 OBTAINING BY FRAUD 1ST (§44 -53-40) {0-2yrs &or $0-500}
0027 DRUGS-ATTEMP/CONSPIRACY (§44-53-40) {one half penalty of substantive offence}
0326 RA (§A) {0-1yr &/or $0-5K}
0049 CRIMINAL CONSPIRACY {0-5yrs &/or $0-200}
0891 BREACH OF PEACE {0-30 DAYS &/OR $0-200}

0297 OBTAINING BY FRAUD 2ND (§44 -53-40) {0-5yrs &or $0-2k}
0044 PISTOL {0-1 yr &/or $0-1K}
2364 STOLEN PISTOL or PISTOL BY MINOR {0-5yrs &? or $0-2K}
0256 RA (§B) (0-10 yrs &/or &1K.10K)

All offenses with a possible sentence of 20 years or more are 85% time.

<u>Underline</u> = no suspended sentence or probation may be given.

Contents

Preface

The median age of convicted felons rose from 27 to 29 years of age. But teenage murders were an exception to the trend. Teenagers account for 10% of violent crimes. Yet, the overwhelming majority of America's 27 million youth between the ages of 10 and 17 never commit crimes. The acts of crime are learned behaviors. The basic values, attitudes, and interpersonal skills acquired early in life are likely to be pivotal in developing predisposition for crime later in life.

Today, many Americans area ringing the alarm pedal with regard to crime and the legal system in the United States. Acts of crime are condemned by our society. We as a whole are upset and frustrated by their persistence and frequency. Laws or rules lower the risk of crime. The success of making and enforcing rules depends on the willingness of a population to support and obey. rules.

If we are to survive as healthy, responsible, and caring people, we must teach ourselves and our youth to solve crime through the judicial system and regulatory agencies such as Law Enforcement. We must make every effort to alleviate problems and to increase educational and economic opportunities.

I believe this resource booklet will assist schools, administrators, teachers, parents, and youth as they struggle to cope with the growing problem of crime. I wish I could say this resource booklet will eliminate crime, but it won't! Crime will be with us. However, this booklet will help individuals and groups who want to head-off incidents of crime, 'get a handle' on the problem, and develop policies and procedures to cope with it.

Dr. Joyce A. Miller
Piedmont Community Actions, Incorporated,
Spartanburg, South Carolina
Region IV

Introduction

This resource booklet is for the benefit of individuals, groups, organizations, church congregations, educational institutions, and non-profit organizations, as well as the public at large, to better understand the present criminal justice system. There are many laws, rules, and guidelines that the general public may not know or of which it may not be aware. Compiled in this booklet is valuable educational information on law enforcement.

The cost of enforcing laws, the building of more facilities of incarceration, more arrests and inmate maintenance have caused a serious outcry from the public in general. This booklet explains some of the problems related to questions of arrest and law enforcement policy that may not be generally known — how the criminal justice system works with regard to arrest, bond hearings, sentencing, probation and parole, plus much more. Should someone you know ever be arrested, the information in this booklet will be handily available.

Law Enforcement and Judicial System Information

Section I:

Criminal Justice System

Richard L. Robinson

Four Major Components[1]

Law Enforcement: Responsibility — Prevention of crime; investigation of crimes, and apprehension of criminals within our society.

Detention Facilities: Responsibility — Detain accused persons prior to trial and in some cases, for short-sentence confinement and rehabilitation.

Courts: Responsibility — Determine guilt or innocence, type and length of sentence.

Corrections: Responsibility — Long-term confinement and rehabilitation.

Note: These four components of the criminal justice system must cooperate closely with each other for the system to work smoothly and efficiently.

---

[1] Johnson, Ricky, Director - South Carolina Criminal Justice Academy, *Jail Officer Training Manual* Chapter 1 —American Jail: Its Origins and Development, page 1.

Arrest[2]

There are four sets of circumstances under which a law enforcement officer may make an arrest:

1. An offense is committed in a law enforcement officer's presence. If an officer has personal direct knowledge of a crime, an arrest may be made without first obtaining an arrest warrant.

2. An officer has "Reasonable Cause" to believe that a felony has been committed and that the accused committed that felony. The officer may arrest the accused without a warrant.

3. The officer investigating a crime determines who he reasonably believes committed the crime and obtains a warrant to arrest from a Justice of the Peace or a judge before making the arrest.

4. An officer is directed to arrest someone on a warrant issued by a judicial officer and based upon a citizen's sworn complaint. The officer will be given a warrant when sent to make the arrest.

---

[2] Johnson, Ricky, Director - South Carolina Criminal Justice Academy, *Jail Officer Training Manual,* Chapter 3 — Litigation Procedure, page 1

Criminal Justice System Terminology[3]

Burden, of Proof: A requirement to present evidence that will convince the judge or jury of the truth or validity of a charge or allegation. The *Burden* usually falls on the Prosecution [or Plaintiff]. The law may require a party to establish a fact by a *"Preponderance of the Evidence"* or by *"Clear and Convincing Evidence,"* or it may require *"Proof Beyond a Reasonable Doubt."*

Capital Crime: Definitive term for a crime for which the punishment may be death.

Civil Rights: Those *Rights* due from one individual citizen to another, deprivation of which is a civil injury for which redress may be sought in a civil suit.

Civil Suit: A legal proceeding by one party against another to enforce a right, to protect property, or to redress or prevent an injury. Judgment for the Plaintiff requires that the defendant perform an act or pay money in damages rather than be imprisoned as in a criminal case.

Class Action: A lawsuit filed by a Plaintiff on behalf of everyone in the same situation or class to redress an injury by a defendant. If the Plaintiff wins, everyone in the "Class" benefits by the judgment. A Plaintiff may also file suit against one named defendant and the Class he or she represents, so that if the Plaintiff wins, he or she may collect from the named defendant and all others in the defendant's Class.

Complaint: 1. The first legal paper filed by a Plaintiff in a civil suit that describes the actions of which complained. It must state a cause of action or it is subject to demur [objection].

2. The document filed by a law enforcement officer or a citizen describing a crime and the person suspected of committing it,

Conspiracy: An agreement plus an overt act between two or more people to commit a crime.

Defendant: One against whom a cause of action or a charge is brought.

Deposition: A written testimony of a witness under oath before trial after giving notice to the opposing party so that he or she [and/or personal attorney] may attend, enter objections, and cross- examine.

---

[3] Johnson, Ricky, Director - South Carolina Criminal Justice Academy, *Jail Officer Training Manual,* Chapter 3 — Litigation Procedure, pages 23-24.

Diversion: Finding alternatives to formal action in the criminal justice system.

Felony: A serious crime that is punishable by incarceration in a State or Federal prison facility [usually for more than 1 year], and or a fine.

Grand Jury: A jury selected to examine the validity of an accusation prior to trial.

Indemnify: To secure [a person] against legal responsibility for actions.

Indictment: A written accusation issued by a Grand Jury to a court, charging a named individual with a crime. The accused is said to be "indicted". The Grand Jury-holds hearings at which the Prosecutor presents evidence against a suspect. If the Grand Jurors decide that the Prosecutor has sufficient evidence to warrant a trial, an indictment is issued.

Litigation: A contest in court; a lawsuit.

Miranda Warnings: A criminal defendant's constitutionally protected rights to remain silent, to have the presence of an attorney before and during any questioning, and for an attorney to be appointed if the defendant is indigent [unable to pay for the services of a personal attorney].

Misdemeanor: A minor criminal charge punishable by incarceration in a city or county detention facility, rather than being incarcerated in a prison, for less than 1 year, and/or a fine.

Plaintiff: A person who files a lawsuit against another.

Probable Cause: Facts that would lead a reasonably intelligent and prudent person to believe that a crime was committed and that the suspect committed it, sufficiently to justify an arrest or a search.

Punitive Damages: Damages awarded by a jury to punish the civil defendant and deter others. In most jurisdictions, neither cities nor insurance companies can indemnify an officer for punitive damages, and they cannot be discharged through the Bankruptcy Courts.

Recognizance: A written promise by a prisoner to appear in court whenever so ordered. Criminal defendants in some jurisdictions are released on their own recognizance pending trial instead of being required to buy bail bonds or to post bail [cash or securities] to secure their release.

Right Against Self-Incrimination: The Fifth Amendment — the right of an accused not to be compelled to testify against self or to produce personal papers or documents that might tend to incriminate himself or herself.

Right to Counsel: The Sixth Amendment — the right of an accused to have attorney representation "at every critical stage" of a criminal proceeding.

Subpoena: A command from a court of law or other body ordering a witness to appear and to give testimony — imposing a penalty for refusal. Subpoena may include an order to bring certain documents into court.

Summons: A call by an authority such as a judge to appear at a specified place before a court of justice.

True Bill: A Grand Jury indictment.

Important Incarceration Information

Release Requirements:[4]

a. Post entire *Surety Bond* in cash, [Surety Bond is the cash value amount set by a judge for a defendant to be released from a detention facility until the court trial date.]

or

b. Ask a relative who resides in same town or city, to sign the Surety Bond — using their home or properties as collateral to match the monetary value of the Surety Bond. Should a relative so choose, he or she assumes responsibility that the accused will appear on the court date or will lose the collateral claims on the Surety Bond,

or

c. Pay a professional Bail Bondsman. This entails an agreement to pay a percentage fee for the Bail Bondsman to assume responsibility for ensuring that the accused will appear in Court as stipulated on the Surety Bond. The fee of a Bail Bondsman usually ranges from 10% to 15% of the Surety Bond's cash value.

or

d. Personal Recognizance Bond [PRB] — A judge may allow an accused person to sign a Bond that states that he or she [the accused] is released on own recognizance pending the trial and will appear in Court whenever ordered, rather than the accused being required to buy Bail Bonds or to post bail [in cash or securities] to secure release.

Incarceration:[5]

a. Most detention facilities have a form on which an inmate may report grievances or may make special requests with regard to a specific problem or condition while incarcerated.

b. A Grievance/Request Form may be used to convey a written message to medical staff, the Magistrate Court, the Circuit Court, the Public Defender's Office, the Solicitor's Office, the Warden or Director of the Facility, or to other staff at the Detention Facility relative to a specific problem with the criminal charges or to housing. A response will be returned to the inmate on the same Grievance/Request Form, usually within a week's time.

---

[4] Johnson, Ricky, Director - South Carolina Criminal Justice Academy, *Jail Officer Training Manual*, Chapter 1, pages 7-9: Release of Inmates [Code of Law Section No. 2-5351 of the American Correctional Association Standards].

[5] Johnson, Ricky, Director - South Carolina Criminal Justice Academy, *Jail Officer Training Manual* — Chapter 2 Legal Rights Within the Corrections Environment, pages 10-13.

c. An inmate may request representation by a Public Defender attorney by filling out a Grievance/Request Form.

d. An inmate may receive visits from a personal attorney or from a Public Defender representative by formally or informally scheduled appointments.

e. A Grievance/Request Form may be filled out by an inmate for forwarding to his or her Public Defender representative, the Solicitor's Office, a Magistrate Judge, a Circuit Court Judge, [etc], to request a bond reduction of the Surety Bond cash value so that the amount may be affordable to secure release until court date.

f. Prescription medications and prescription eyeglasses of inmates may be brought to them from home by someone. Detention Facility staff will get them to the inmate.

g. Inmates may sign up for Visitations Privileges so relatives, friends, and clerics or pastors may visit them. Ask Detention Facility supervisors about the Facility's Visitation Policies.

h. Detention Facility staff may be asked by an inmate for the current list of registered Bondsman. Generally each lobby or cell area has a Bondsman List available for the telephoning convenience of inmates.

i. Individuals may bring money to the Detention Facility for an inmate and leave it at the specified lobby area or may send a United States Postal Money Order [in the name of the inmate] to the Detention Facility address.

j. Most Detention facilities provide blankets, towels, face cloths, mattress covers, pillows, underwear, personal hygiene items such as toothpaste, deodorant, soap, comb, razor and blades for shaving.

k. Personal items — clothing, property, forms, money — may be released to a designated person by signing a Personal Property Release Request Form which [by permission of the inmate] grants release of all personal property listed on the form to the person designated.

Booking and Warrants[6]

Booking

a. When being "Booked" into a Detention Facility, an arrestee must be sure to answer all questions truthfully and in good faith on any form presented to him or her, especially with regard to questions on property, money, and medical information. Before giving the form or information to Detention Facility staff, arrestee needs to examine and re-check all answers for accuracy and then, to sign in the appropriate signature space.

b. Arrestee will be allowed a phone call after he or she has been Booked into the Detention Facility, to inform family or friends of whereabouts.

c. Arrestee's parents or friends may call the Detention Facility telephone number to be informed of the Surety Bond amount for release of the inmate or when he or she may appear before a Magistrate Judge for Bond Arraignment. [A *Surety Bond* is a cash value obligation that is placed on an arrestee's Booking Card, along with other statements or conditions under which an arrestee may be released from a Detention Facility until Court date set by the Presiding Judge.]

d. If another Detention Facility has a Hold Lien on an arrestee's booking card, the arrestee may be detained from being released. [A *Hold lien* on a Booking Card is a written statement or teletype information that requests retention of an arrestee for further Warrants to be served from another jurisdiction or law enforcement agency.

Warrants

a. A Warrant is an arrest document that states criminal offenses that are charged against an accused.

b. The Warrant Department of each law enforcement agency is responsible for serving Arrest Warrants to individuals, groups, or organizations that have been accused of committing a crime. Arrest Warrants are served by official Law Enforcement representatives and may be hand delivered to a home address whether the intended person is there or not. As long as there has been an attempt to contact the person, that person is liable for the Warrant.

c. If an arrestee has a previous General Session Court date, he or she must take care of this important matter by contacting the Solicitor's staff by letter or by phone. Failure to notify the Solicitor's Office of previous Court date may cause a **Bench Warrant** to be issued against the accused while he or she is being detained in a Detention Facility. [A *Bench Warrant* is an Arrest Warrant that is served on an individual, group or

---

[6] Johnson, Ricky, Director - South Carolina Criminal Justice Academy, *Jail Officer Training Manual,* Chapter 1, pages 1-4: Admissions, Records, and Release {Code of Law Section No. 2-5099, 2-5101, 2-5102 of the American Correctional Standards].

organization that fails to appear in Court at the originally set date and time, and may result in a fine or jail time.

Arrest Warrant?

Reasons for an Arrest Warrant

An Arrest Warrant serves as a legal Law Enforcement document and is signed by a Presiding Judge. It is to prevent or discourage an accused from committing bodily harm, stealing, or damaging personal property.

Steps in Obtaining an Arrest Warrant

Step 1: Report a crime to the nearest Law Enforcement agency for investigation. Ask Law Enforcement Officer for a written *Incident Report* which details the matter. if injury has occurred, a medical report is required from the attending hospital or clinic with a copy to the Magistrate Office.

Step 2: Go to the Magistrate Office with the written report of the incident, received from the Law Enforcement Officer. There, another form must be completed that states in a narrative summary, who, what, when, where, and how this incident occurred. The written Incident Report and the form containing the narrative summary will be submitted to the Presiding Judge for review.

Step 3: A Magistrate Judge will read and ask questions about the information provided on the Incident Report and the Narrative Summary form. If the incident merits an Arrest Warrant, a Clerk of the Court will prepare a brief Incident Report that states the charges contained in the Arrest Warrant.

Step 4: The Arrest Warrant will be signed by a judge, making the Warrant official, after which it will be passed to the Warrant Division to be served by a Law Enforcement Officer. The Law Enforcement Officer will have two copies of the Arrest Warrant: one for the Court system and the other for the accused.

Step 5: An Accused will be arrested by a Law Enforcement Officer after the charges in the Warrant have been read aloud to the person. The arrested person will be properly handcuffed and escorted to a Detention Facility for a Bond Arraignment Hearing of the criminal charges.

Arrestee Behavior[7]

Behavior

a. All rules for the guidance of inmate behavior must be followed and obeyed.

b. While in a Detention Facility, a Detention Officer is the immediate supervisor of an inmate at all times, and all direct orders from a Detention Officer must be followed and obeyed by the inmates — no exceptions.

c. Any serious violations of the rules or inappropriate inmate behavior may result in an appearance before the In-House Disciplinary Committee. This Committee consists of staff members and officers who will determine which privileges may be restricted should an inmate behave inappropriately.

Criminal Offense Charges — Driving

Driving Under the Influence of alcohol *[DUI]* or Driving Under Suspension — without a license *[DUS]*. Third offenses on either of these charges may cause a person to serve time in a Detention Facility or to do *"Weekend Time."*

A Weekender generally serves 48 hours per weekend [Saturday and Sunday], and is housed at a Detention Facility. Such an arrestee performs work on highways and other community or township work. Weekend inmates receive credited days toward their sentenced time each weekend that they report for duty according to the Weekend Sentence guidelines of the Detention Facility.

Criminal Offense Charges — Domestic Violence

A Third or fourth offense of this type may require an appearance before a General Session Court with possible sentencing or Probation with an attached fine. [A Criminal Domestic Violence offense is a criminal charge that involves parties living in the same household fighting, pushing, or arguing with each other in a violent way.] [See page47]

---

[7] Johnson, Ricky, Director - South Carolina Criminal Justice Academy, *Jail Officer Training Manual,* Chapter 2, pages 10-13: Classification Upon Admission and Regulation of Behavior of Inmates [Code of Law Section No. 2-55347, 2-55348, of the American Correctional Standards].

Bond Arraignment[8]

Generally for Bond Arraignment, an arrested person will be called to appear before the Magistrate Court's Presiding Judge for that particular day. The Bond Arraignment is a brief and limited hearing by a Presiding Court Judge who listens to and hears the criminal charges brought against an arrestee. The Magistrate Court Judge makes a decision on the information presented to her or him from the Arrest Warrant with regard to the conditions for the arrestee to be released from the Detention Facility until the Court appearance date.

a. A Magistrate Court judge holds Bond Arraignments at designated and set periods of time, usually every 4 hours or every 6 hours within a 24-hour time period. Relatives of friends of an arrestee need to call the Magistrate Court or Detention Facility to inquire about the time set for the Bond Arraignment Hearing.

b. The Presiding Magistrate Judge will review each of the Arrest Warrants charged against an arrestee, plus any previous criminal charge warrants on an arrestee's present or past Criminal Record File. An Arrestee's file will be pulled from the Detention Facility's records and will be placed on the Presiding Judge's desk for review.

c. Detention Facility staff will be informed by the Presiding Magistrate Judge when to have the arrestee in the Court Room for the Bond Arraignment Hearing.

d. Before deciding and setting the amount of the Surety Bond, the Presiding Judge will review the files of the arrestee's information folder and will ask questions relative to the current Arrest Warrant charges and any past related charges.

Terms related to Bond Arraignment Hearings

Surety Bond   A Surety Bond consists of a cash value obligation placed on a detainee's Arrest Booking Card by a Judge stating the total cash amount that the detainee must pay to be pre-released from a Detention Facility until date of Court appearance set by the Presiding Judge. The arrestee may need the assistance of a Bail Bondsman or of an immediate family member to post bail for his or her release. The Presiding Judge will inform the arrestee during the Bond Arraignment of the kind of service required in order to be released [the services of a Bondsman or that of a relative] as stated on the Arrest Booking Card. Usually a Presiding Judge will place a high Surety Bond on Arrest Warrant Charges such as Armed Robbery, 1st and 2nd Degree Burglary, Inciting to Riot, Kidnapping, Murder, Aggravated Assault, Criminal Sexual Conduct, Drug Trafficking, 1st degree Arson and Strong- Armed Robbery.

---

[8] Johnson, Ricky, Director - South Carolina Criminal Justice Academy, *Jail Officer Training Manual,* Chapter 3, pages 15-24: Litigation Procedure.

Personal Recognizance Bond [PRB]

Is a Surety Bond by which an arrestee is released on his or her own recognizance pending trial rather than being required to have a Bail Bondsman to post bail [cash or securities] in order to be released from a Detention Facility. Usually the Presiding Judge will allow a First-Time Crime Offender to sign his or her own Surety Bond if the person is a taxpayer who has been a resident of that town or area for a specific period of time [usually over a year], and has a steady job or occupation. Personal Recognizance Bond may be set on Arrest Warrant Charges such as Driving Under the Influence [DUI] of Alcohol, After such an arrestee has been detained for 4 hours in a Holding Cell at a Detention Facility, he or she may be released after the Bond Arraignment Hearing.

A person arrested for DUI may be signed out by a personal attorney who will be held responsible for driving the client home. Examples of other Arrest Warrant charges for which a PRB may be set are: Leaving the Scene of an Accident, Battery, Carrying a Concealed Weapon, Disorderly Conduct, Gambling, Offering to Commit Prostitution, Possession of Marijuana, Possession of Drug Paraphernalia, *Petit* Theft [under $1000 cash value], Trespassing, and the Writing of Worthless Checks which are Misdemeanor charges.

A minimum amount of Surety Bond is usually set for the above types of charges.

Signed Bond

A Surety Bond that is signed by a member of the arrestee's immediate family [defined as a brother, sister, mother or father] who is willing to offer their land, property, or house deed as collateral toward the cash value of the Surety Bond amount set by the Magistrate Judge for release of the arrestee from a Detention Facility until the date of the Court hearing.

Out-of-Town Arrests[9]

When a person is arrested [for traffic violations or other Criminal Offense Charges] while out of town, the following important facts in obtaining release from an out-of-town Detention Facility may prove helpful.

a. If arrestee doesn't have enough money to pay the total amount of the Surety Bond for bail as stated on the Arrest Booking Card, the arrestee may call a Bail Bondsman that handles out-of-town clients, or the arrestee may call a close relative or friend to pay the bail amount to the Western Union office nearest the Detention Facility in which the arrestee is being held. A staff member of the Detention Facility will take receipt of the bail cash on behalf of the person being detained.

b. While being housed in a Detention' Facility, a detainee may call or write to a close relative or friend, asking that a United States Postal Money Order in the amount of the Surety Bond be sent or delivered to the mailing address of the Detention Facility. When the amount of the Bail Bond has been received at the Detention Facility and deposited in its Fund Account, the detainee may use these funds toward release, after notification of a staff member or supervisors of the Detention Facility.

c. A Chaplain at the Detention Facility or immediate staff supervisor may be asked for additional assistance or information with regard to being released from the Detention Facility.

---

[9] Johnson, Ricky, Director - South Carolina Criminal Justice Academy, *Jail Officer Training Manual,* Chapter 1,pages 1-4: Admissions, Records, and Release [Code of Law Section No. 2-5099, 2-5101, 2-5102 of the American Correctional Standards].

Accuracy of Information[10]

It is extremely important for an arrestee to give the Arresting Officer and the Detention Booking Officer very accurate information when asked. The information that an arrestee furnishes for the Arrest Booking Card is the exact information that the Detention Facility and the Court judges will use relative to the arrestee's criminal Warrant charges.

    a.   On the Arrest Booking Card, an arras tee must be sure that his or her name is spelled correctly, address is correct, age, date of birth, race, sex, height and weight, color of hair and eyes, etc, is accurately given and recorded.

    b.   Additionally an arrestee must check the correctness, on the Arrest Booking Card, of the following information: Social Security Number, Driver's License Number, next of kin's correct address and telephone number, in case of emergency.

    c.   The Arrestee must also ascertain if all Arrest Warrant tickets have been accurately listed on the Arrest Booking Card.

    d.   It is also the responsibility of the arrestee to verify that Court dates listed on Warrant tickets relative to traffic violations, fines pending, etc, have been or are entered on the Arrest Booking Card.

---

[10] Johnson, Ricky, Director - South Carolina Criminal Justice Academy, *Jail Officer Training Manual,* Chapter 1, pages 1-4: Admissions, Records, and Release [Code of Law Section No, 2-5039, 2-5101, 2-5102 of the American Correctional Standards].

Roll Call[11]

The term "Roll Call" means the calling of the names of the inmates for summary appearance at a General Session Court before a Sentencing Judge who will decide the court date.

a. An arrestee must report and be present on the appointed date of the court hearing related to his or her Criminal Arrest Warrant Charges as listed on the Surety Bond from the Magistrate Court.

b. All questions asked by the Presiding Court Judge must be answered. The Presiding Court Judge will have Arrest Warrant copies available for the Sentencing Judge to review.

c. Failure on the part of the arrestee to be present or not being available when the names are called by the Presiding Court Judge may result in the arrestee having a Bench Warrant served against him or her.

   [1]   A Bench Warrant is an Arrest Warrant issued by a Presiding Court Judge on an arrestee who fails to appear or to answer the scheduled court date for sentencing based on the criminal Arrest Warrant charges.
   [2]   Arrestees also must contact the Solicitor's Office for clarification on the Court Roll Call system procedures for General Session criminal Arrest Warrant charges.

---

[11] Johnson, Ricky, Director - South Carolina Criminal Justice Academy, *Jail Officer Training Manual,* Chapter 3, page 15: Litigation Procedure.

Bench Warrants[12]

A Bench Warrant is an Arrest Warrant issued and signed by a judge of one of the following courts: Magistrate Court, Circuit Court, Family Court, or Traffic Court. A Bench Warrant is issued for an arrestee who fails to appear on the scheduled date for court, trial, roll call or a hearing of the charges on a criminal Arrest Warrant. The court system issues Bench Warrants for arrestees to assure that all arrestees who have criminal Arrest Warrant charges against them will eventually be tried and sentenced accordingly.

a. A Bench Warrant generally states the original Arrest Warrant charges and the date issued with imposed sentence and fines set by the judge who presided on the original court date.

b. Most Bench Warrants state the conditions set by the Presiding Sentencing Judge and the requirements an arrestee must meet or honor to be released from the Detention Facility.

c. **Types of Bench Warrants**

[1]   Magistrate Court Bench Warrant A Bench Warrant that is issued and signed by a Magistrate Court Judge for an arrestee who fails to appear in court at the date and time previously scheduled. A Magistrate Court Bench Warrant is usually issued for charges such as Trespassing, Disorderly Conduct, simple traffic violations [Misdemeanor], *Petit* Theft, the writing of worthless checks [Misdemeanor], Simple Assault, and Check Fraud.

[2]   General Session Court Bench Warrant

A General Session Court Bench, Warrant is issued and signed by a Circuit Court Judge, Family Court Judge, or Traffic Court Judge for an arrestee who fails to appear for Roll Call on the date and time of the appointed date for a Hearing related to the charges noted in the criminal Arrest Warrant. Generally the Presiding Judge imposes a sentence and orders the arrestee to be held in a Detention Facility until the next scheduled Hearing date as set. This type of Warrant is usually issued for criminal Arrest Warrant charges such as: Failure to pay child support; Armed Robbery; First and Second Degree Burglary; Kidnapping; Murder; Criminal Sexual Conduct; Drug Trafficking; First Degree Arson; Aggravated Assault; and Aggravated Child Abuse.

An arrestee must appear on the appointed court date or face a Bench Warrant from the court system. The arrestee is responsible for this date — *not* the personal attorney.

---

[12] Johnson, Ricky, Director - South Carolina Criminal Justice Academy, *Jail Officer Training Manual,* Chapter 3, pages 15-17: Litigation Procedure.

Preliminary Hearing[13]

A Preliminary Hearing is a pre-court Hearing related to an arrestee's criminal Arrest Warrant charges. The purpose of the Preliminary Hearing is to determine whether there is "Probable Cause" to believe that the accused committed the crime with which he or she has been charged. The Preliminary Hearing provides the accused an opportunity to obtain an advance look at the evidence that the Prosecution intends to present against them at trial.

a. During Bond Arraignment Hearings for arrestees, the Presiding Magistrate court Judge will tell each arrestee if he or she qualifies for a Preliminary Court Hearing relative to their Arrest Warrant charges.

b. If an arrestee qualifies, the Presiding Judge will issue a Preliminary Hearing form to be filled out and mailed to the Magistrate Court within 10 days. the accused probably will receive a reply within 2 to 3 weeks from the Magistrate Court with an assigned date and time for a Preliminary Hearing.

c. If there is not enough criminal evidence against the accused to show "Probable Cause", Arrest Warrant charges may be dismissed by the court system.

---

[13] Johnson, Ricky, Director - South Carolina Criminal Justice Academy, *Jail Officer Training Manual,* Chapter 3, page 15: Litigation Procedure.

Pre-Trial Intervention[14]

A Pre-Trial-Intervention Program is a program administered by the Solicitor's Office staff to help First-Time Offenders of non-violent Arrest Warrant criminal charges [such as Shoplifting, Violation of Gun Act, Breach of Trust, some Drug Possession charges, Forgery] to receive reduced sentence time and fines — a one-time court 'deal' approved by the Solicitor's Office and the Court System.

Sequence of a Pre-Trial Intervention Sentence

[a]   Arrestee would ask personal attorney to contact the Solicitor's office about the Arrest Warrant charges for consideration for Pre-Trial Intervention.

[b]   Arrestee would file an application with the Solicitor's office for Pre-Trial Intervention Program. Filing fee: $50 or more — dependent upon where arrested [city, county, state]. The total Pre-Trial Intervention cost may be as much as $350.00 without the services of an attorney.

[1]   A Pre-Trial Intervention Program consist of the arrestee receiving counseling services, assignment of community work service, and fines.

[2]   Original Arrest Warrant charges may be dropped from arrestee's criminal record file by the Solicitor's Office after certain conditions are met and approved by the Solicitor's staff and the Court System. For example: a person charged with possession of an illegal substance may receive a fine and the assignment of a definite number of hours of community service to be completed before he or she would be eligible for release.

---

[14] Johnson, Ricky, Director- South Carolina Criminal Justice Academy, *Jail Officer Training Manual,* Chapter 3, pages 20-25: Litigation Procedure.

Detention Facility[15]

A Detention Facility is a jail that houses arrestees for the different cities, hamlets, and townships that comprise a particular county or boundary area until Bond Arraignment Hearings, Court Trials, or Hearings and Sentencing occur.

a. Many local townships in this country house arrestees in their local jail holding cell areas until arrestees have been booked-in and the township is ready to transfer them to the detainees to the country Detention Facility until Bond Arraignment.

b. Detention Facility advantages

Helps reduce housing and operational costs for individual townships.

   Speeds-up Bond Arraignment of arrestees.

   Proximity of Detention Facility to Court House is usually closer, making it easier for Law Enforcement agencies to transport inmates to Court.

Escape-prevention building structure, design, location, and security staff of Detention Facilities facilitates the housing of criminals with all types of Arrest Warrant charges.

---

[15] Johnson, Ricky, Director - South Caroline Criminal Justice Academy, *Jail Officer Training Manual,* Chapter 1,
pages 1-10: The American Jail: Its Origins and Development.

A Warden[16]

A Warden is the person in charge of the management and supervision of inmates [with short- or long-term sentences] who are housed in a Detention or Correctional Facility under his or her jurisdiction. The Warden is also in charge of the supervision of the Law Enforcement staff of the Facility.

a. Detention Facility Wardens are appointed by County Council Selection Board Members.

b. Wardens of Correctional Facilities are appointed by State Correctional Commission Board Members.

Warden Responsibilities

a. House and secure inmates.

b. Manage Law Enforcement staff who are directly responsible for the safekeeping of inmates.

c. Account for expenditures related to food, clothing, personal hygiene items, medical costs, etc, for the inmates housed in the Facility under his or her jurisdiction.

---

[16] Spartanburg County Detention Facility Policies and Procedures Manual, Section I — Management: Director, pages 6-10, [Code of Law Section No. 2-5006 - 2-5010 of the American Correctional Association Standards].

Bail Bondsman[17]

A Bail Bondsman is a person or agency registered with the Clerk of the Court and that is licensed by the Criminal Court System to provide bail service for arrestees and inmates. Bondsmen may be called on to assist in gaining the release of an arrestee from a Detention Facility until the appointed date to appear in court.

Generally, the more serious the criminal offense, the more likely the Magistrate Judge will require a bail amount to be posted by a locally based registered Bondsman.

After a Bondsman has signed to post the bail amount of the Surety Bond to obtain release of an arrestee until the court appointed date, the Bondsman is held responsible for the released person to appear in court on the dated scheduled.

Most Bondsman charge clients a fee of 10% to 15% of a Surety Bond's total amount. Most Bonds-men are insured for $10,000 or more in equity [cash and property value] to post bail amounts for clients as stipulated by the Clerk of the Court.

As an individual, one of the advantages of utilizing the services of a Bondsman is that personal property is not at risk in order to secure the release of an inmate from a Detention Facility. If an arrestee or an inmate fails to appear in court on the appointed court date or "skips town", the Bondsman is held responsible for getting that person to court or forfeits cash that has been registered with the Clerk of the Court until that person does appear in court.

---

[17] Johnson, Ricky, Director - South Carolina Criminal Justice Academy, *Jail Officer Training Manual*, Chapter 3 -Litigation Procedures — Bail, page 15.

Legal Representation for An Arrestee[18]

An Arrestee may require the legal services of a personal attorney or the services of an attorney of the Public Defender's Office to represent him or her in General Session Court to answer Criminal Arrest Warrant charges such as Aiding Escape, First and Second Degree Burglary with Aggravating Circumstances, Armed Robbery, Kidnapping, Murder, Criminal Sexual Conduct, Voluntary Manslaughter, Drug Trafficking, First Degree Arson, etc.

An attorney from the Public Defender's Office is appointed by the State on behalf of an arrestee or inmate to provide legal representation in the Court System. An arrestee or inmate may qualify for this type of legal service if his or her personal income is no more than $125 per week or gross income does not exceed $6000 per year. There is a $25 Application Fee if the arrestee or inmate can afford to pay it, as determined by the Public Defender's Office.

Note: While incarcerated, an inmate must make copies of all arrest warrant papers in his or her possession, available for reading and review by a personal attorney or an attorney from the Public Defender's Office prior to the Hearing or Sentencing court date.

An inmate may acquire copies of any documentation that pertains to his or her criminal case and may review additional information from the Law Library of the Facility in which being housed. In most Detention or Jail Facilities, this information may be acquired through a visit to the Facility's Law Library or by completing a written request form.

---

[18] Johnson, Ricky, Director - South Carolina Criminal Justice Academy, *Jail Officer Training Manual,* Chapter 2 -page 10-13: Legal Rights and Responsibilities Within the Corrections Environment.

Medical Costs for Inmates[19]

Detention Facilities and Department of Correctional Facilities are obligated, according to the Criminal Justice Court System, to furnish inmates with medical treatment of health or dental conditions while incarcerated, if needed.

Each local jail, Detention Facility, Correctional Facility, and Law Enforcement Agency has a separate budgeted allotment for medical and dental costs. In South Carolina, the Medical Budget includes staffing costs for the medical and dental personnel who serve the inmates within the Facility.

In my hometown of Spartanburg, South Carolina, the County Detention Facility has an inmate population of approximately 600. Its operational medical costs for inmates housed there easily exceeds $400,000 per year, including the cost of salaried medical staff.

South Carolina Department of Corrections has an estimated annual medical budget of $28 million dollars to cover an average population of 17,500 inmates housed in the different county Correctional
Facilities and sites.

---

[19] Johnson, Ricky, Director - South Carolina Criminal Justice Academy, *Jail Officer Training Manual,* Chapter 2 -Legal Rights and Responsibilities Within the Corrections Environment, page 10.

Work Status of Inmates[20]

Inmates awaiting court dates or sentencing in County Detention Facilities cannot be forced to participate in Work Programs outlined by the Detention Facility. The Eighth Amendment protects the right of an inmate to refuse to participate in an institutional work program while being detained. However, inmate who have received sentences and are serving their time in a Department of Corrections or Detention Facility must participate in the rehabilitation and work programs offered.

Many Detention Centers and Correctional Centers have classification procedures — decisions on housing, work, and program assignments, and recommendations for the handling of inappropriate behavior in sentenced inmates.

Many Detention and Correctional Facilities make credit hours available to sentenced inmates for earned "good time". If the behavior and work performance meet "good" standards as recorded in the Policy and Procedures Manual, "good time earned credit hours" are logged for inmates. These earned credit hours help reduce the number of days to which an originally sentenced — possibly early release from the Detention or Correctional Facility.

Job Assignment Lists are available in some Detention and Correctional Centers from which sentenced inmates may choose in order to earn "good time" credit hours.

---

[20] Johnson, Ricky, Director - South Carolina Criminal Justice Academy, *Jail Officer Training Manual,* Chapter 2 - Legal Rights and Responsibilities Within the Corrections Environment, pages 12-13.

Attorney Fees[21]

All arrestees have legally protected rights of access to court, attorneys, and to legal materials.

A Detention Officer may not prevent an inmate from seeking judicial relief for his or her complaints. If an inmate cannot afford a personal attorney for representation in court to answer Criminal Arrest Warrant charges, the State will hire an attorney to represent the person.

The State of South Carolina pays $60 per hour for a State court-appointed attorney to represent a defendant who cannot afford a private lawyer. If a Public Defender is not available for the court date[s], many other attorneys charge a fee of $100 or more per hour for "talking sessions."

Some Public Defender Offices charge a $25 Application Fee for a defendant who cannot afford a private attorney while incarcerated.

---

[21] Johnson, Ricky, Director - South Carolina Criminal Justice Academy, *Jail Officer Training Manual,* Chapter 2 -Legal Rights and Responsibilities Within the Corrections Environment, page 11.

Prison Population

"Rising Inmate Population Sparks Boom in Construction"[22]

Many States believe there is no choice other than to build more prison sites because of the over-crowdedness of the prisons in their areas. Corrections officials gained approval to build 213 State and Federal prisons built between 1990 and 1995 to cope with the quickly expanding inmate population that now exceeds — for the first time — one [1] million [reported by the Justice Department and quoted by Associated Press Reporter, Cassandra Burrell.

As of June 30, 1995, State or Federal Correctional Facilities held 1.02 million people — that figure up from 715,649 in 1990, as stated in a statistical report. To accommodate the increase in prisoners, 168 State and 45 Federal prisons were built to increase the number of such institutions to 1500. The number of prison beds rose 41% to an estimated 976,000.

Estimations are that State prisons operated at an average 3% over capacity, and Federal prisons were 24% over capacity. By 1995, about half of the State and Federal prisons were more than 20 years old, and nearly 40% of inmates were incarcerated in Facilities built since 1985. The inmate population had risen to 409 inmates per 100,000 County resident population by 1995, and figures released this year [1997], places the number for 1996 at 427 inmates per 100,000 County residents, according to a report by Department of Justice statistician, James Stephan.[23]

---

[22] Burrell, Cassandra — Associated Press, Spartanburg Herald Journal, August 8, 1997, Section A-4. Stephan,
[23] James — Department of Justice statistician quoted in the Burrell article referenced above.

General Juvenile Policy[24]

A "juvenile" is classified as an individual under the legal age of seventeen, and may be detained in a Detention Facility according to the State law of that area with the approval of the Family Court System. Juveniles who are ten [10] years of age or younger will not be detained in a Detention Facility under any circumstances. Juveniles between the ages of eleven [11] and twelve [12] years may be detained in a Detention Facility but only by order of a. Family Court Judge.

The Department of Juvenile Justice is the agency responsible for deciding whether to release or detain juveniles who are taken into custody by Law Enforcement agencies in cases other than violent offenses, as defined by State Law Enforcement policies. If a juvenile is charged with criminal offenses such as Murder, Voluntary Manslaughter, Armed Robbery, First Degree Arson, First Degree Burglary, or Drug Trafficking, the Department of Juvenile Justice shall obtain the consent of the appropriate Law Enforcement agency prior to the release of the juvenile offender.

If a juvenile has been arrested for criminal charges, the arresting officer will notify an agent of the Department of Juvenile Justice for that specific area to come to the Detention or Jail Facility to assist in the completion of the Booking and Screening process of the juvenile offender who will be temporarily housed at that Facility. The agent of the Department of Juvenile Justice will be responsible for contacting the parents of the arrested juvenile offender.

a. Unless otherwise ordered by the court, a juvenile offender shall be released to the custody of his or her parents, guardian, custodian, or to others as designated by the court.

b. A juvenile offender shall not be held in a Detention Facility any longer than forty-eight[48] hours excluding Sundays and Holidays unless an order for such detention is signed by a judge of the Family Court.

c. After the initial forty-eight [48] hour detention, a juvenile offender shall not be held longer than seven [7] days without a Court ordered extension. Additional extensions, not to exceed seven [7] days each, may be made by subsequent orders of the Court. Such orders shall be in writing.

d. A juvenile offender shall not serve a sentence exceeding thirty [30] days in a local Detention Facility.

---

[24] Johnson, Ricky, Director - South Carolina Criminal Justice Academy, *Jail Officer Training Manual,* Chapter 5, page 11: Admissions, Records, and Release [Code of Law Section No. 1040 of the American Correctional Association Standards].

Criminal Domestic Violence[25]

Of all women who visit Hospital Emergency Rooms, 20% to 35% are there for Domestic Violence-related injuries. Battering is the leading cause of injury to American Women. Domestic Abuse is the cause of more injuries to women than Rape, Muggings, and automobile accidents *combined.* Criminal Domestic violence is a criminal Arrest Warrant charge that involves parties who are living in the same household, fighting, pushing, or arguing with each other in a violent way such that a Law Enforcement agency must intervene.

Criminal Domestic Violence charges may be served in a relationship of boyfriend and girlfriend, or husband and wife wherein physical or bodily harm occurs within an argument or dispute.

a. A Criminal Domestic Violence Arrest Warrant may be served when pushing, cursing, fighting, or other physical or bodily harm occurs.

b. Either of the parties involved may go to a Magistrate officer to file charges for a Criminal Domestic Violence Arrest Warrant to be served after reporting the matter or incident to a local Law Enforcement agency for investigation.

c. Second offense Criminal Domestic Violence charges may result in a larger fine or possible sentence of over ninety [90] days in jail. Third or fourth offenses of Criminal Domestic violence may result in an individual appearing in a General Session Court.

---

[25] Parker, Kathleen, Spartanburg Herald Journal, Opinion Column - September 3, 1997 edition.

Parole and Probation Guidelines[26]

Parole: The release of an inmate before his or her full sentence has been served, conditional on good conduct.

Probation: A period of suspended penalty; a period of time during which an offender must report at regular intervals to a Probation Officer after being released from jail or a Correctional Facility.

After hearing the pre-Sentencing Arguments, a Presiding Judge has alternatives in making a decision:

a. Sentence may be suspended:
b. The Defendant may be placed on Probation with required performance of certain obligations by the Defendant under the supervision of the Court's Probation Officer; or
c. The Defendant may be sentenced to a term in either a Detention Center, a Reformatory, or a Correctional Facility.

After a Defendant has served any imposed minimum sentence, he or she would normally become eligible for Parole. The decision to actually grant Parole is generally made by the State Parole Board of a State, based upon the Defendant's record while imprisoned. A Parolee is supervised by a Parole Officer of that agency.

Different distinguishing features of Probation and Parole:

Probation is granted as a result of pre-conviction behavior; Parole is granted, in large measure, on post-conviction behavior.

---

[26] Johnson, Ricky, Director - South Carolina Criminal Justice Academy, *Jail Officer Training Manual,* Chapter 3 -Litigation Procedures, page 17.

Emergency Situations[27]

Should an emergency situation occur while a family member is incarcerated; locally or while out of town, the following information may be of service.

Locally:

When an emergency situation or a matter that is life-threatening [such as news of a serious illness or serious car accident, etc] needs to be reported to an inmate who is being housed in a Detention or Jail Facility, a member of the inmate's family [specifically: a mother, father, brother or sister, daughter or son] may call the particular jail facility and ask to speak with a Supervisor who is On Duty.

The Supervisor On Duty will probably ask questions about the situation and may request a telephone number or address in order to be able to get back in touch with the caller after making inquiries about the matter. After verifying the information, the Supervisor On Duty will call back and will also get in touch with the inmate. The related Facility Policies and Procedures will be explained by the Supervisor to both the inmate and family caller at a convenient time.

Out of Town:

If a serious event occurs while an inmate is being housed in another County or State jail facility, the inmate may inform the Staff Supervisor on duty at the Facility and ask to speak with the appropriate staff [usually a higher authority position] to request guidelines on the proper procedure to be followed in that Facility. The appropriate person may be the Warden, a Major, a Lieutenant, or a Sergeant at the Facility.

a. For an emergency visit to a hospital, the transport of an inmate, from either a Detention or Correctional Facility, by a staff member, must be approved by one of the higher-authority positions noted above within the approval guidelines set by that particular hospital or agency that the inmate is going to visit for an emergency visit to a family member. The inmate probably will be allowed between 30 and 60 minutes visitation time with the family-member patient at the hospital; The inmate will be fully restrained and escorted by a Facility Officer.

b. The transport of an inmate by a staff member from either a Detention or Correctional Facility to attend the funeral of a family member also requires approval by a higher-authority staff member as noted above. Most Detention or Correctional Facilities allow an inmate one of two choices:

[1] Attend the Quiet-Hour Vigil, or

---

[27] Johnson, Ricky, Director - South Carolina Criminal Justice Academy, *Jail Officer Training Manual,* Chapter 2 -Legal Rights and Responsibilities Within the Corrections Environment, pages 10-13.

[2] Attend the actual Funeral-Burial.

For further information on inmate hospital emergency visits and funeral attendance procedures, a family member may contact the Facility within which the inmate is being housed.

"Special Information"

Preliminary Hearings

By law, necessary witnesses must appear at a preliminary hearing in order to show that the defendant(s) probably committed the offense charged. You should also bring with you any medical reports, bills, canceled checks, repair estimates, or other documents that tend to show the extent of your injuries or damages.

By law, the defendant or his attorney may question witnesses who testify at a preliminary hearing but cannot testify or call witnesses.

Unless prior arrangements have been made with the solicitor on this court, all necessary officers, affiants and other witnesses must be present at the time set for the preliminary learning or the case may be dismissed.

Unless prior arrangements have been made with the solicitor or this court, all defendants or their attorney's must be present at the time set for the preliminary hearing or the hearing will be waived.

"Special Information"

Subject: Home detention program (An alternative to incarcerations for low risk, nonviolent adult and juvenile offenders) "As selected by the court if there is a home detention program available in the jurisdiction" As an alternative to: (1) Pretrial or preadjudatory detention (2) Probation (3) Community corrections (4) Parole (5) Work release (6) Institutional furloughs (7) Jail diversion (8) Shock incarceration program for people awaiting trail and for offenders whose sentences do not place them in the custody of department of corrections. All family court offenders committed to the jail must be made eligible for the home detention program by the presiding family court judge. All home detention programs must be approved by the jail staff. Home detention criteria as list below as outlined for this program.

(1) Voluntary participation (2) Agreement by the participant to pay all program fees (3) No pending criminal charges (4) No history of escape, criminal domestic violence or extensive criminal history involving crimes of violence (5) Compliant behavior and adherence to jail rules (6)

Permanent county residence (7) Valid employment (8) Installation of telephone and adherence to regulations concerning use of telephone (9) Consent of other residents residing in participant's home/residence (10) a. Other criteria as outlined b. Failure to agree or comply to the terms of the program will result in the individual's removal from the program, and the individual return to the secure custody of the jail.

Important Special Facts On Legal Law Matters

Child support payments must be paid to the Family Court on scheduled time or arrestee could be facing sentence time:

A. Sentence time guidelines for first time offender for non-payment of child support could range from 90 days to 6 months.

B. Second offense for non-payment of child support sentence time guideline ranges from 6 months up to 1 year.

C. Child support payment fee could range as low as $30.00 per child per week up to $150.00 per child per week based on your total income.

D. Arrestee child support payment fee obligation accumulates on while being incarcerated in jail or the detention center. That back time child support payment fee must be paid to Family Court sometime with a specific allocated time, set by the presiding Family Court judge when arrestee is released from the jail or detention center.

E. If arrestee somehow loses his job or gets l aid off while paying child support payments, need to notify Family Court immediately.

   1. Arrestee needs to try to get child support payments reduced according to his new income or work out arrangement of paying back time child support payment with a Family Court judge.

   2. If arrestee has a reduction in income wage relating to his present job, need to contact Family Court immediately to apply for child support fee reduction payment arrangement.

If you were ever arrested or a family member was arrested on a serious criminal arrest warrant charge, you have a choice of having a public defender or private attorney to represent you in court according to your financial income.

A. Public defender attorney representing you may cause you to stay in jail or detention center for a long period of time before your criminal arrest warrant charges are heard by the court system, usually within 90 days up to one year or longer.

B. Private attorney represents you, could have your criminal arrest warrant charge be heard by a court system usually within two weeks or 30 days.

Be able to contact department head of the public defender office, need to address this matter to Chief Public Defender.

Be able to contact department head of the Magistrate court office, need to address this matter to Chief Magistrate Court.

If someone you know has been arrested that needs drugs or mental health treatment, etc., you need to contact that arrest officer, presiding judge who will be in charge of seeing his arraignment bond hearing. Also contact Probate Judge for further assistance relating to this matter.

All victim witness persons must be notified when a bond arraignment hearing has been scheduled against the arrestee warrant person by the jail or detention center staff. Also must be notified when that arrestee will be released from jail or detention center, by telephone.

Post Conviction Review is an appeal word term that a prisoner who is served a long sentence time in the Department of Correctional Center may want to apply for in hoping to receive reduced time sentence or being released from prison.

1. **Post conviction review can be filed only by someone actually serving time in prison.**

2. **Post conviction review can only raise constitutional defects.**

3. **Post conviction petitions can bring up case issues not discussed or raised during the first actual trial, place constitutional protections rights that have arisen up since the original trial.**

4. **Inmate or prisoner can file numbers of petitions for post conviction review at all levels of the court system.**

5. **Post conviction review prisoner may use a private attorney or public defender attorney tore present him in court on this matter.**

Important Court Legal Information Tips Services

Magistrate Court Bench Warrant Fines must be paid at Magistrate Court Office to a assigned clerk personnel or to a magistrate judge on duty. Make sure you get a paid receipt copy back.

Traffic court bench warrant files must be paid at traffic court office to a assigned clerk personnel or to a traffic court judge on duty. Make sure you get a paid receipt copy back.

Child support bench warrant fries must be paid at family court to a assigned clerk personnel or to a family court judge on duty. Make sure you get a paid receipt copy back.

You must have a paid receipt from these bench warrant lists above to show payment of proof to be able to get someone release out of jail or detention center at Magistrate Court Designated Office.

You may want to call the jail or detention center facility or Magistrate Court office to get information about bond arraignment or release information relating to your loved ones, friend, family members, etc. Who has been arrest on a criminal warrant charge. This will save you time, money and traveling expense and also will help you toward making some kind of wise decision how to handle this legal court arrest charge matter.

To get help for a loved one for immediate family member that has a serious problem relating to drag abuse, alcohol abuse, mental abuse, etc. You may want to contact a detoxification center in your living area, also you may want to make contact with the Probate court to see a probate judge in issuing a retainer arrest warrant paper on the loved one immediate family member to be picked up and transported to the local area hospital for treatment and evaluation help. The Sheriff's Department or your local law enforcement agency will transport that individual there. You may have to pay a minimum service fee to the probate court office for this service for your family member.

To have someone subpoenaed to court as a witness for you relating to your arrest warrant charge you need to inform the judge to have subpoena papers served on them. This need to be done five days before trial date.

Section II:

Opinion Briefs

Richard L. Robinson

Violent Crime Control and Law Enforcement Act

The Violent Crime Control and Law Enforcement Act is a law about offenses committed by juveniles — making it illegal to sell or give a gun to a juvenile for use. The only exception is for the purpose of hunting.

The State of South Carolina found 202 guns in the State school system during the official school year of 1996. The education officials believe that there were more instances which were not reported. Law Enforcement Agencies believe that guns are more plentifully available among youth than ever before. Children who are armed today are younger than the children who were caught carrying guns 5 years ago.

Children were protected from the availability of guns in the past when settling arguments, fights or disputes with parents and neighbors. But in today's society, it seems that more children are being killed or injured by guns. Parents and neighborhoods need the same cooperation they had in the past in dealing with these problems. Working together collectively in the development of good moral standards, and working habits for children in the neighborhoods could make this society a better place in which to live and prosper.

Visitation Privileges for Inmates

It is my opinion that inmates deserve visitation privileges with family members, friends, or ministers while incarcerated. The number of visits are decided by the Detention Facility Director or Warden in accordance with guidelines set by the Department of Corrections Commission based on the State Criminal Judicial System Code of Law.

Visitation Policies are usually stated in a manual written by the Warden or Director of the Facility for staff and inmates, and are used as guidelines in the form of an informational booklet that states the security conditions under which visits may be made to inmates on specific dates and times, and specifying personal appearance, apparel and clothing, proper identification, age requirements, etc. The guidelines also state how long the visit may last.

Special note: No one under the age of seventeen [17] years of age may legally visit an inmate without being accompanied by one of his or her legal parents. Usually there are Visitation Forms available for inmates to fill out listing the names of those they wish to visit them during that week. Unless a person's name is listed on the Visitation Form, that person will not be allowed to visit the inmate. There are no exceptions unless approved by the Warden or Director of that Facility.

Personal Privileges for Inmates

Inmate privileges help ease some of the built-up tension that occurs from being incarcerated. Personal privileges include: being allowed to visit the Canteen to purchase something sweet as a snack or to purchase cigarettes and to have smoking privileges; watch television; play cards; use the telephone to make calls to relatives and friends at designed assigned time; and being allowed to use a Recreation Area at designated assigned times to play basketball or sports for exercise. Some detainees and inmates become more relaxed in an incarcerated environment when allowed such privileges.

The Canteen of many Detention or Correctional Facilities stock additional personal hygiene items such as soap, toothpaste and brushes, deodorant, etc, for purchase by inmates. Writing materials, envelopes, pencils and pens for onsite use are also available for purchase by the inmates.

Recently there was discussion on local radio talk shows about the fact that inmates are allowed to earn a maximum of $36 per month at present [1997], but there is a law soon to take effect that will not allow any payment for work done during incarceration. When that law becomes effective, inmates will no longer be able to earn the money to purchase personal items such as for hygiene, snacks, smoking, writing, etc.

Parenthood and Crimes

In today's society there are more single parents than there were a century ago. Divorces have tripled. Single-parent household populations have doubled in size. It seems that pressure from our society related to moral values, money and drug abuse problems have contributed to the single-parent status in this nation.

With the increase of more single-parented families there has been an increase in juvenile crimes and situations related to the Criminal Justice System. Availability of working parents and quality time at home for childrearing is becoming increasingly difficult. Many children of the ages classified as being "juvenile" are becoming more involved in serious criminal events such as Burglary, Carrying Concealed Firearms, Murder, Drug Possession, Trafficking, and Criminal Sexual Conduct. It has been estimated that the Criminal Justice System sustains a cost of $30,000 per year to house, feed, and secure each juvenile offender in a Department Of Justice Juvenile Housing Facility.

It seems in today's society that there is a need to help improve the relationships within single parent households. Maybe more role models within our society such as Teachers, Ministers, neighborhood residents, Law Enforcement officers, may help reduce the tendency of our children to commit crimes and may deter the breakup of family units.

Appointment of Judges

Many people are not aware of how judges are appointed to serve in the Local, State, and Federal Judiciary Systems. Judgeships in some States are appointed by Elective General Assembly Representatives and members of the State's Congress [State House of Representatives and State Senate]. A Governor of a State may also appoint persons to particular judgeship positions. For specific information on how certain judicial appointments are made in your area, and what the qualifications and Terms of Reference are for the different positions, the following may be contacted: the Governor of the State, Mayors of cities, City Council Members, State Senators, State House of Representatives Members.

Most Federal Judgeship Appointees are recommended by State Governors with the approval of both Congressional Houses of Representatives and the Senates of the State and Federal Government Levels.

Inmates and Institutionalization

"Institutionalization" is a word that makes me feel very uncomfortable. But many Repeat Offenders are facing this situation of becoming "Institutionalized" because they feel quite secure within the jail environment, and believe that the Criminal Justice System will take better care of them than their own community as far as food, clothing, housing and accommodations, dental and medical assistance being provided to them as needed.

Mentally and physically, many Repeat Offenders are prepared to do their sentence time for criminal charges that have been brought against them.

In some States, the Criminal Justice System requires inmates to earn a "GED" Diploma — an educational certificate — and to learn a job skill before being released from a Correctional Facility, with the hope that the education and training will deter them away from "Institutionalization."

The Work Ethic and Repeat Offenders

Many Repeat Offenders are unable to hold a steady job for at least six [6] months of a year. Some of them have drug and alcohol related problems of have health problems.

It is expensive for society and the Criminal Justice System to overlook this matter. Here are two ideas offered for the consideration of the community and the criminal Justice System.

1. Family Sponsorship Program for Repeat Offenders in which a set allowance would be given to a family that would be responsible for assisting a Repeat Offender to find a job, a place to stay and reliable transportation to work for a trial period of at least one [1] year. A Family Sponsorship Program would be cheaper than paying out an estimated amount of $13,000 a year to house each Repeat Offender in a Detention Facility.

2. Funding of Halfway Houses by Churches and other non-profit organizations or agencies to assist Repeat Offenders to find a job, housing, and transportation to and from work for a trial period of at least one [1] year per sponsored offender.

Fraudulent Checks

On most Fraudulent Check Arrest Warrants it is stated that the amount the offender owes on each overdraft check. Copies of each individual overdraft check from each purchase or payment are attached to each Fraudulent Check Arrest Warrant. [*Fraudulent Check* is defined as proceeding from fraud, given to using fraud, deceitful, dishonest as related to money.]

The Magistrate Court generally handles Fraudulent Check Arrest Warrants, and will probably demand full payment of the amount on all returned checks with proof of restitution on each check that is an overdraft, plus Court costs. Court costs vary within each State. On most Fraudulent Check Bench Warrants, the jail sentence noted in days may be stated on each individual overdraft check, if the offender fails to pay the correct amount on each overdraft check used to make purchases or payment, plus payment of the Court costs.

Any sentence time over ninety [90] days may result in serving the time in a Department of Corrections Facility.

Special Note: If a letter or notice about an overdrawn check has been sent, there are about 10 days allowed to take care of this matter before the business or individual to whom the over draft was written may request a Fraudulent Check Arrest Warrant.

Nonpayment of Child Support

In most instances of Nonpayment of Child Support Arrest Warrants, the exact amount the arrestee is behind in Child Support fees is noted along with the date that it is due to be paid to the Family Court System. A Nonpayment of Child Support Arrest Warrant is issued only when there is failure to pay Child Support money on time according to the Family Court Order. Most Family Court Systems charge a 3% Collections fee on the gross amount of each individual Child Support check. Collection Fees generally go to the County Reserve Funds Account.

a. To stay out of jail and not face sentence time by a Family Court Judge, all Child Support payments must be paid promptly as ordered.

b. Child Support payments are handled by the Family Court Department.

c. Failure to pay Child Support payments that are in arrears may result in a Family Court Bench Warrant being served with legal possibility of jail time until an appointed Court Hearing date is set by a Family Court Judge.

Special Note: Anyone who pays monthly Child Support fees must pay those fees to the Family Court Unit. At no time should Child Support fees be paid to the beneficiary in cash because there would be no proof of payment — unlike payment by check or money order. If cash payment is made, it is probable that no payment will be credited for that month's Child Support fee by the Family Court.

It is necessary that Child Support payments be made to the Family Court so the correct money amount may be deposited to the child's or children's Support Fee Account. The Family Court will withdraw the money by check and will send it to the mailing address of the correct beneficiary.

Repeat Offenders and Sentences

Question:

Should violent offenders serve longer sentences after two or three repeated felony convictions?

Citizens of many States are pushing the Judicial System to 'hand down' longer sentence times for convicted Repeat Offenders of violent felonies. Correctional Institutions in many States have some of the same basic problems: the heavy burden of housing costs for long-term inmates. Many State prison facilities would actually double in size if longer sentence times were imposed on violent repeat offenders.

Some States are thinking about re-classifying non-violent offenders such as small-time drug users and other non-violent criminal types into an Alternative Sentence Guideline Program. Some of the Alternative Sentence Programs suggest that non-violent offenders pay restitution to their victims and reimburse the State for their upkeep and Court costs; be placed under house arrest for a certain period of time; and be assigned to a Regional Work Camp for so many hours per day. Such Alternative Programs would help reserve needed space in prisons for those who represent a greater danger to others in our society.

Bench Warrants

How a person may be released from a Jail or detention center if facing the following: Family Court — Child Support Bench Warrant; Traffic Court Bench Warrant; Circuit Court Bench Warrant; or Violation of Probation Bench Warrant.

1   Family Court Child Support Bench Warrant is arrest warrant stating that arrestee has failed to comply with child support payment fees to the Family Court on a weekly or monthly scheduled time period, by order of the Family Court Judge. Arrest Warrant probably will state that the arrestee be detained in jail until a new court trial hearing date has been set by a Family Court Judge or an Arrest Warrant may state payment in full for the child support amount as stated on the Arrest Warrant in order to be released from jail or a detention center.

·   An arrestee could be released from jail or detention center on this particular arrest warrant charge by having someone pay the full child support amount stated on the Arrest Warrant to the Family Court Trial Division.

·   Arrestee may also be released from jail by hiring an attorney to speak on his/her behalf to the judge who issued the Bench Warrant against him/her, and in getting the judge to arrange some kind of revised financial arrangement for the child support payment with a bond set on the Arrestee Booking Card. The arrestee may be able to call a professional bondsman in helping him to be released from jail or the detention center.

2   A Traffic Court Bench Warrant is an arrest warrant stating that the arrestee failed to appear in Traffic Court on the appointed court trial date and time as stated on the traffic ticket or Surety Bond Arraignment document, or if the arrestee failed to pay in full the amount of his Bond Surety as stated on the Arrest Warrant.

·   Arrestee could be released from jail or detention center on this particular arrest warrant charge if someone pays the full amount of the violation fine as stated on the arrest warrant to Traffic Court Division.

·   The arrestee may also be released from jail or detention center through an attorney speaking on his behalf to the judge who issued the Bench Warrant, posing the possibility of a financial arrangement or payment plan, and the setting of a bond amount on the arrestee's Arrest Booking Card. She or he may be able to call a professional bondsman to assist in the release.

3   A Traffic Court Bench Warrant is an arrest warrant stating that the arrestee failed to appear in Traffic Court on the appointed court trial date and time as stated on the traffic ticket or Surety Bond Arraignment document, or if the arrestee failed to pay in full the amount of his Bond Surety as stated on the Arrest Warrant.

An arrestee may be released from jail or detention center by hiring an attorney who would speak on his/her behalf to the judge who issued the Bench Warrant against the arrestee. The judge may allow a bond amount to be set on the arrestee's Arrest Booking Card so the detainee would be able to call a professional bondsman to assist in the release.

The arrestee who cannot afford an attorney to speak to the Circuit Court Judge to set a bond on his/her arrest warrant charge[s] may want to ask for an Inmate Written Grievance Request Form from staff members or the supervisor on duty. This form is for communication to the Circuit Court Office, the Solicitor's Office, and the Public Defender's Office to ask a judge from the Circuit Court to set a bond amount for the release of a detainee.

4. A Violation of Probation Bench Warrant is an arrest warrant that states that the arrestee failed to keep his/her written contractural condition agreement with the Probation and Parole Department. Violations of this nature include such things as not reporting to one's Probation Officer, failing to make restitution payment, failing drug test, not living up to the terms written in an agreement as stated on Probation documents, being involved in a criminal act while out of jail or the detention center.

An arrestee may be released from jail or detention center by hiring an attorney to speak on his/her behalf to a Circuit Court Judge for the setting of a bond amount on the arrestee's Arrest Booking Card, and the arrestee may be able to call a professional bondsman to assist in a release.

General Sessions Cases

Cases usually heard in the General Sessions Court are criminal cases which carry a maximum penalty upon conviction of more than 30 days imprisonment of a fine of more than $200.00 for each offense.

Note: Arrestee Summary Court, Magistrate Court, and Municipal Court cases deal with the same type of warrant charges.

Arrestee criminal cases that carry a maximum penalty upon conviction of not more than 30 days imprisonment or a fine of not more than $200.00 for each offense are usually heard in the Magistrate Courts or the Municipal Courts.

1 If an arrestee's case is not called for trial during his/her first appearance in the General Sessions Court, it will be necessary for the arrestee to attend each succeeding term of court until some disposition is made of the arrestee's case.

2 In General Sessions Court, an arrestee's case will be tried before a jury unless the arrestee requests otherwise.

3 An arrestee is entitled to a jury trial in the Summary Court, but unless the arrestee specifically requests a jury trial before the trial commences, the arrestee's case will be tried before a judge without a jury.

Bonds Set by Circuit Court

Only a Circuit Court Judge may set bonds for Murder, First Degree Burglary, First Degree Lynching, Safecracking, or any other offense that carries a maximum penalty upon conviction of Life Imprisonment — a Summary Court Judge cannot set bonds on those warrant charges. If an arrestee who is charged with the criminal offenses, he/she needs to discuss the matter with an attorney to make arrangements to get a bond set by a Circuit Court Judge.

Fugitives from Justice

If an arrestee has been charged with being a Fugitive from Justice from another State, that other State will request that the Governor of the State [in with the arrestee is charged] turn over the arrestee for trial. This process is called Extradition — a process that usually takes several months. During that time, the arrestee is entitled to bond. If Extradition is granted, the arrestee will be taken to the other State to stand trial for the alleged offenses. If Extradition is waived, the arrestee will be taken to the other State immediately and will not be entitled to bond in the arresting State. Unless the Extradition process is begun within 20 days after the arrest, the arrestee is entitled to be released from jail.

Note:

An arrestee has the right and the obligation to be present at trial. Should an arrestee fail to attend the court, the trial will proceed in his/her absence. An arrestee may also be charged with a separate criminal offense if he/she fails to appear as required by the bond.

Use this convenient coupon for ordering paperback

Mailing Address: Law Enforcement and Judicial System Information Booklet Richard L. Robinson Tips Kid's Care Association PO Box 3446 Spartanburg, South Carolina 29304-3446 (864) 583-5190

Please send me _____ copy/copies of booklet at sales price of $12.95 per booklet. [Please add $3.00 for each booklet to cover postage and handling costs.] Total $15.95 per booklet copy.

Total amount _____order.

Thank you!

Richard L. Robinson,
Executive Director
Tips Kid's Care Association

Send check or money order-[no cash or C.O.D.'s] payable to: Tips Kid's Care Association

Specify for: Law Enforcement and Judicial System Information Booklet
Please allow a minimum of 3-5 weeks delivery

or

Copies of individual chapters or topics [$2.50 per chapter or topic]
Please allow a 2 week postal delivery

Law Enforcement and Judicial System Information Booklet order for the following address:

Ms./Mrs./Mr.   _____

Address: _____

City: _____   State _____   Zip_____

Special note for fund raising events for non-profit organizations! For all non-profit organizations, we will offer a special booklet promotional deal price on Law Enforcement and Judicial System Information Booklet, for your organization in helping you toward raising funds in meeting your financial goals for your organization's budget year.

If interested in this special booklet promotion deal price project for raising funds for your non-profit organization, please contact by letter at the above mailing address. You may include your phone number also.

Your Name _____ Telephone #_____

Name of Non-Profit Organization_____

Address: _____

City: _____ State _____ Zip_____

Telephone   (....)

Thank You!

Re: The Author

Richard Lewis Robinson is a native of Spartanburg, South Carolina. He is the first son of Mr. and Mrs. Willie Robinson; has three brothers and one sister; is married to the former Janette D. Rice of Spartanburg. They have three children.

Mr. Robinson graduated in 1965 from Carver High School [Spartanburg, SC], and attended Morris College in Sumter, South Carolina from 1965 to 1966. He is a graduate of the Art Instructors School of Minneapolis, Minnesota. He received his Art Diploma in 1969, and a degree in Advertising and Illustration. In 1977, Mr. Robinson received an Associates Degree in Business Administration from the Spartanburg Technical College.

A former Sunday School teacher of 10 years for the junior class at Golden Street Baptist Church, Mr. Robinson is currently a member of Bibleway Holiness Church of Inman, South Carolina. He received the Honor Award from the Vogelweh Chapel [Kaiserslautern, Germany] — a certificate awarded by the chapel and staff for faithful service to the community. Mr. Robinson served in the United States Army in Europe [Kaiserslautern, Germany] as a Clerk and Switchboard Operator from 1970 to 1972; was elected as Correctional Office Representative for the Northside Correctional Center [Spartanburg, SC] from 1987 to 1989; served in the 178th Infantry Division of the National Guard [Spartanburg, SC] from 1989 to 1991, as a Cook. In 1990, Mr. Robinson served as President of the Bethlehem Center Parents and Teachers Club [Spartanburg, SC].

In the Spartanburg [SC] area Mr. Robinson has held such positions as Commercial Artist for Cryovac, Division of W.R. Grace Corporation for 10 years; was a Correctional Officer at Northside Correctional Center, a Minimum Security Institution for 3 years, and has been employed for the last 10 years at the Spartanburg County Detention Center as a Detention Officer Corporal.